for the spirit horses.

To Diane
in Word & Spirit

Spirit Horses
(c) Al Hunter, 2002. All rights reserved.
First Edition

Cover Design: Austin Graphics
Cover Image & Inside Artwork: (c) 2002 Leo Yerxa. All rights reserved.

Kegedonce Press
Cape Croker Reserve
R.R. 5 Wiarton, Ontario N0H 2T0
Phone/Fax: 519 534-5107
Email: renee@kegedonce.com and kateri@kegedonce.com
Website: www.kegedonce.com

Member of CanCopy

Editor: Kateri Akiwenzie-Damm
CIP
Canadian Cataloguing in Publication Data

Hunter, Al, 1958 -
Spirit Horses
Poems.
ISBN 0-9697120-8-1

I. Title.
PS8565.U5767S65 2001   C811'.6   C2001-903104-1
PR9199.4.H85S65 2001

Kegedonce Press gratefully acknowledges the support of the Canada Council for the Arts.

Acknowledgments

I would like to thank the Creator and the spirits who send the words and messages and bring them to life through voice. Thanks and love to my family, especially, my late father, Albert Hunter Sr. To Andy, Graham, Emily, Joey, and Katie, I give my love and devotion. I give thanks to Elijah, a light when it gets dark. I extend my gratitude to Kateri Akiwenzie-Damm and Kegedonce Press for publishing this work, for faith, friendship, and boundless patience with me and a manuscript that have gone through many transformations and fits and starts. Thanks also to Leo Yerxa for the gift of having his artistry accompany this work. I thank the Canada Council for the assistance to publish this book.

Many, many thanks to Heid Erdrich who took the time to give thoughtful, insightful and encouraging comments to drafts as they emerged. To Malcolm "Mac" O'Neill-Fischer, I also say thanks, for providing compassionate and helpful proofreading and editing whenever I asked. Thanks also to "Cody", four year old Arabian stallion, for sharing his gifts of presence and spirit and to Joanne & Kent Ogden of Aurora Wind Arabians and Bill Morgenstern of Earth Moods for making it happen.

I would like to acknowledge and thank my friends for their faith, friendship, encouragement over the years. I offer my sincerest thanks to Sister Mary Richard Boo, John Schifsky, Mary Curtis, Greg Wilson, and Leonard Peel, teachers in my past, who each in their own way and time taught me to glimpse the value of words and expression. Miigwech to all who participated in A Walk To Remember: A Sacred Journey around Lake Superior during the summer of 2000, especially, the children.

To those friends and teachers who gave and taught me so much over many years and who have since passed on to the spirit world; Randy Councillor Sr., James Leonard Sr., E.K. (Kim) Caldwell, Ron Geyshick, Walt Bresette, and Alexandra Smith, I say, miigwech and aangwaamizin, thanks and take care.

Over the years, I have found much inspiration, strength, affirmation, and courage in the words and works of Louise Erdrich, John Trudell, Joy Harjo, James Wright and Hermann Hesse, and in the messages and dreams sent by the spirit horses.

Finally, I would like to thank Sandra Indian, (Spirit Horse), whom I met at a sacred fire and, for whom, a flame will forever show the way.

Spirit Horses

Horses In My Heart

In Neah Bay 10
Feather Poem 11
Many winters 12
Letter Mailed, Posthumously 13
Desert Solo 17
Where is the moon? 19

Storm Dancers

Poem for Patrick Eller 22
On The River 23
The One Who Climbs Hills 24
The Light 25
Storm Dancers 27

Heart Listeners

Prayer Bowl 30
Breathing Butterflies 31
The Spirit of Creation 32

Horse Sense

Breathe 34
Ghosts on the rock 35
Clear cut 36
Horse Sense 37

Blue Horses

Blue Horses 40
Finding Pablo 41
from the chambers of a ragged heart 42

Passages 43
Rattling the bones 44
Jailer 45
The Union 46
After the Solstice 50
Hummingbird 52

Migrations

Migrations 54
Equinox II 58
Recent Visitors 59
Shake the feathers 60
Egress 62
Spring Run 63
April Rising 65
The Way It Is 66

Legacies 67
Still 68
Dance of the Trees 69
Altered 70

Dream Horses

RedHawk, BlueSky,
where have you gone? 72
Seven Horses 82
Horsecoat 83
Dream Horses 84

Horses in My Heart

In Neah Bay

for Spirit Horse

1.
To say that there are words to describe the feelings of the ocean would be to lie. To
use a language that would describe one ounce of ocean wave would be to speak the
tongue yet to be spoken. There are no words.

horses in my heart.
horses in my heart.

2.
From the farthest northwest corner of this island,
of this continent, the blue sea -
emerald tides and waves of jade,
touching and caressing ancient faces of the land.
I dream of you. I think of you. I remember you.

Feather Poem

Perhaps it was the Leonard Cohen
But at 9:53 tonight
I want to call
for your embrace
or a caress of words to fill this lonely cup
I want to call
to tell you that I need your arms
to embrace me like wings
to feel your heart singing
a warm and tender bird
calling me to alms.

Perhaps it was your letters
your letters that traveled to these trembling fingers
to these hands, to these eyes, to this heart, to this man
reaching out
giving alms
gasping
as whispering feathers fall
like fading songs
from a warm and tender bird
already taking wing.

Many winters
for Barb

looking west
across the fields

how deep the snow is
how deep the snow is

to traverse the distance

between us

how deep the winters are
how deep the winters are

Letter Mailed, Posthumously

> Trying to forget -
> The hardest part of trying to forget
> is the remembering forgetting brings back.
> - John Trudell

I

It is a quarter to five on the second last day of December. It's almost dark. Still, there is enough light to discern the silhouette of the trees - the poplar, the birch, the willow, the elm and the ash.

Even in the approaching darkness, the sky is strangely blue - pale, dusty blue. Depending on what kind of day it is, the snow will appear to be blue. Sometimes, it can even be a wide open, bright, sunny day or at that moment just before darkness falls.

Yesterday, last night, this morning, tonight, the trees are tinged with frost. When I close my eyes, I can remember the scene behind my house, looking over the rock that sits silently, calmly like a guardian. My mind and heart can remember. And then, there are the trees. My favourite is the tall, old poplar standing there like a brother.

II

The images in my mind of the sun rising visibly beyond the trees, over that standing brother, over that old, guardian grandfather, remain vivid and strong. The images in my mind help me to remember the trees, the land, the rocks - help me to remember not to forget.

Forgetting is easy. It is the remembering that is hard. Or is it the forgetting that is hard and the remembering that is easy?

I am remembering the trees, the rocks, the colours, the sky, the snow, the cold, and the promise of another, new day. I am remembering the sun, rising again, a silent, magnificent promise of light.

Sometimes it's so hard to find the solitude to be able to remember. . . . Sometimes, even to forget.

III

It's supposed to be the fourth day of January. Happy New Year.

IV

It is the fifth day of January. Outside, it is bright and blue. It looks cold. This morning, telling the dreams aloud, I was nervous. Until that point, I was able to keep them tucked away, silent, fragile and tender. Now, they are no longer silent, though they maintain their fragility, their tenderness.

Dreams. When to speak of them - that is the challenge sometimes. There is such a thing as speaking too soon, too late, not at all, or when the time is right. It felt like the time was right.

I have dreamed of you. I told these dreams of you, to you, tenderly, gently, without any pretense or hesitation. They are gifts. As you would behold the person, you behold the dream, until the feelings are inseparable - for the person, for the dream, both beautiful, both needing tenderness and grace, honour, and respect.

V

This morning I rose at five-thirty. It is now seven-fifteen on the sixth day of January. There is such beautiful light at this time of the day. I remember an elder telling me, *The trees are feathers.* As I look east through the window in my door, this is the thought that returned to me - *The trees are feathers.* They do look like feathers! Even without their leaves! Feathers give life. Trees give life. Both provide protection. Both listen. We forget sometimes that we have these helpers and givers and protectors of life all around us, always with us.

It feels really good to get up before anyone else is up in the house. It provides an opportunity to pray, to meditate, to just be with my Creator. The communion feels stronger at this time of the day. The praying and meditating relax me. It will help me to meet the day and whatever this day happens to bring with it.

You are in my thoughts and prayers this morning. Your presence is always with me. We are so connected. It amazes me. Your thoughts and words constantly touch me. Your compassion gives hope.

VI

It is nine days into January. Lying here in my bed looking north, it appears to be misty and lightly raining.

Often I wonder why we find it so easy to find despair or to create despair in our lives. We are so good, so practiced at creating fiction from illusions - other people's illusions, illusions that keep us prisoners from ourselves, within ourselves. We need to write, to tell, to sing, to pray, to dance, to scream, to yell, to rejoice, to recite, to incite, to chant, to cant, to speak our own stories, even if it means creating our own fiction from our own illusions.

Why do we wait? The longest journey is from the head to the heart.

VII

It is twenty days into January. The snow, the frozen bands and ridges, forms and ripples, remind me of a porcelain landscape prepared to crumble at the lightest touch.

The sky is completely blue this morning. It's bright and extremely cold. Inside me, it's warm - my inner landscape carved by blowing winds that did not cease until today. Today, I am able to observe these waves and bands, ridges and forms, ripples and porcelain, able to feel the stillness inside of me. Yet, the cold is always present - ready to frostbite an ear, a finger, or some part of me left exposed.

The sky and my inner landscape, open, expansive, and blue.

Lyrics from "I Went So Willingly" copyright by John Trudell from the release "Tribal Voice" The Peace Company 1983

Desert Solo

for beloved friend and ally, Alexandra Smith, who walked into the spirit world while on a trek through the desert in Mauritania, West Africa on April 12, 2001.

Water, water, water
blue rivers of time still flow for you
laughing stars of heaven still glimmer for you
green oases of refuge still stand for you
infinite eyes of fire still see for you
singing shadows of earth still move for you.

Water, water, water
beneath the earth
above the earth
around the earth
on the earth
in the earth
of the earth
still moves for you
still moves for you
still moves for you
still moves for you.

Water, water, water
blue rivers of time still flow for you
laughing stars of heaven still glimmer for you
green oases of refuge still stand for you
infinite eyes of fire still see for you
singing shadows of earth still move for you.

Water, water, water
still moves for you
still moves for you
still moves for you
still moves for you
on shimmering rivers of stars
on dancing ribbons of northern lights
on spirited wings of thunder
on sacred shores, on sacred shores. . . .

Water, water, water
still moves for you
still moves for you
still moves for you
still moves for you.

Where is the moon?
for my beloved.

Where is the moon tonight?
Is it shining in Paris, blue?
Is it shimmering over the hill in Surrey?
Is it full and blazing orange over the upper peninsula and the eastern horizon near White Pine?
Is it half-full near the edge of that particular northeastern Minnesota town?
Is it just a sliver in the southern sky somewhere near that roaming river in Nebraska?
Is it prairie blue behind a wailing wall of snow and memory in Bismarck, North Dakota?
Is it an upturned bowl waiting to be filled at the limestone edges of LaCrosse?
Is it hanging low just outside that barroom in Eau Claire?
Is it the last quarter lying on the stone and pebble beaches of Grand Marais?
Is it barely visible through the trees in the backwoods near that place in Sawyer County?
Is it a flickering searchlight in the untouched forest of those boundary waters north?
Is it rising over the oak and sugar maple hills where prairie meets clay at White Earth?
Is it hiding behind the curtain of that hotel at the foot of the thunder mountain?
Is it climbing the steep hills of the fabled Meech in that place they call Quebec?
Is it being pierced by that spire on the shores of that roiling Lake Ontario?
Is it shining outside that lonely room near where the rapids roar?
Is it lying at the feet of a broken window in the central hills of that twin port town?
Is it reflected in your wondering eyes?
Where is the moon tonight?
Is it in the wandering ice - on the jagged shores of your beloved?

Storm Dancers

Poem for Patrick Eller

A tattered chapbook with a wolf and three moons -
"the sky full of miracles and everyone is sleeping. . ."

One of the three moons, the largest one, encircles the image
of a bird in flight. The wolf stares off as the second moon
touches his right ear.

The other moon rests over his back, suspended, in the night sky.

Are you the flying bird inside the blue ring of the shining moon?
Are you one of these moons? Which moon are you?
The voice whispering into the ear of the wolf?
The waiting moon above the forest?

On The River

I have been long between landings
Sometimes glimpsing a distant shore
All the while the sounds of rushing rapids grows.

The One Who Climbs Hills

Along trails and creeks that wind through trees, stand hills that wait.
Crowned with pine and sky and wind,
they bask in the warmth of the sun,
sometimes bask in the falling rain,
sometimes bask in the breath and bluster of the wind,
all the time waiting.

The Light

The smoke rising from my neighbour's chimney
informs on the wind coming from the north.
The smoke puffs up,
creating a small cumulus cloud on the rooftop.
It swirls, lies flat with the wind,
then rises,
as if it can barely breathe,
as if there is barely enough air
to sustain it,
to make it rise
and swirl.

There is no frost on the poplars or the birches.
They stand there, bare, still, and silent.
Cold brothers of the forest –
fingers brittle and tender from the wind.

The higher the sun rises,
the wider the shower of light
spreads out over the snow.
The snow, freshly fallen,
takes away the harshness
that has been there.

The sky is wide open and blue –
light blue, almost white
toward the southeast,
as the skies above the other horizons
become deeper and deeper blue.

All needing to be warmed by light.
Fingers, hands, arms, legs,
bodies, hearts, spirits –
all needing to be warmed by light.

Neither surrounded, nor captive,
nor bare, nor silent, nor still.
All needing to be warmed by light.

Not just the reflection of light.
Not just the reflection of light.
Not just the reflection of light.

Storm Dancers

Each night, the storms will dance magnificently across the sky. Lightning
and thunder will sing upon the drum of the earth. The rains will cleanse
the circle. Hail will pelt the helpless, outside. And, each morning,
like an anxious spectator, the sun will rise early onto the shoulders
of the eastern sky to survey and warm the dancing grounds.

Niimig! Niimig! Dance! Dance! He'll urge.
But the dancers and singers will have all gone home.

Heart Listeners

Prayer Bowl

When the moon is turned upwards like a bowl waiting to be filled
We must fill it. We must fill it by honouring the spirits of creation
With songs of our joy and thanks, with foods created with our own hands,
Water for the thirsty, prayers for the people, prayers for the spirits,
Prayers for the Creator, prayers for ourselves, and the sacred instruments
That join us to the glory of this world, that join us to the glory of this world
And to the world beyond our sleep.

Breathing Butterflies
for Ron Geyshick

This morning I dreamed
a veil of butterflies
of all different hues and places
swept into my path
entering my eyes, my ears, my mouth,
until it seemed the butterflies
became my breath.

I swept my arms out, at first afraid
of suffocation, until, giving in
to the utter breadth and mass, a swath
of butterflies so thick, I could barely move.

I kept walking, sometimes waving my arms
lightly, brushing the butterflies away from
my mouth and nose so that I could breathe.
I kept walking on this path until the veil of
butterflies began to thin.

I remember wanting to walk through them
again. I wanted them to come back. I wanted
them to lead me onward, somewhere.

The Spirit of Creation

The spirit of creation
is alive.

It pulsates in time
with the heartbeats of those
who listen with their hearts.

You are a heart listener.
The earth's heart is your heart.

Horse Sense

Breathe

The trees
stripped of cover
sway under the breath of this cold
October sky
spindly fingers grasp at wispy
swift-moving clouds
in a sky
deceivingly blue.

Ghosts on the rock

carved in stone
apparitions breed hard fear

fissures that hide them
are deep
no one knows how deep
some say to the sea
same say below
granite spirits walking
precipices, ledges
cliff sides, rock faces
until they fall
to the chisels
of archaeologists
and rock climbers

Belay the ghost.
Belay the ghost.

Clear cut

You lay the ground open
clear down to the bones of the earth
clear down to the bones of my ancestors
leaving scars
within the boreal forest of your self
stripping away
what you cannot understand
beneath the healing canopy of trees
leaving parts of you bleeding and bald
in your old seasons of promise and plunder
scarred by your own hand.

Horse Sense

Tasting the promise of life
and retching at the poisoned table of the industrial horsemen
I have instead learned of the sanctity of all beings.

Playing with fire
and getting burned by the visible flames of the lying horsemen
I have instead learned of the teachings of providing for life.

Dazzled by bells and whistles
and momentarily blinded by the profits of the neon horsemen
I have instead learned to see the truth of prophecy.

Listening to the language of doublespeak
and almost deafened by the words of the warring horsemen
I have instead learned to listen to spirits.

Beguiled by the perfume of success
and almost consumed by the acrid smell of the chemical horsemen
I have instead learned to walk on this earth.

Blue Horses

Blue Horses

My lover gave me a turquoise-blue horse.
I held her in my outstretched arms and I wept.
For so long I have waited for you, I whispered.
For so long I have dreamed of you, I confided.
For so long I have sung without you, I chanted.
For so long I have prayed without you, I murmured.
For so long I have walked without you,
        I breathed.

Finding Pablo
Valentine's Day

Who are we to think that we might return
to our somber palace of dreams and secrets,
decorated with dusty curtains and old indiscretions?

Who are we to think that we might return to
refurbish our dark grandeur, veil for saboteur and philanderer,
whispering in the dark behind a mirror and a cigarette?

If we believed in love, if we believed in the words of Neruda,
we might have believed, we would return, changed, ourselves.

from the chambers of a ragged heart

It seems that one of my valves has been sticking. I was thinking perhaps it might have something to do with recurring murmurs. Sometimes I wake from dreams asking, sometimes demanding: *Why? Why do you still enter my days and nights after all these years?* Sometimes my heart races in my sleep as we almost meet, eyes searching. Always there is someone nearby, leaving scarcely a moment to ask the questions that lie unanswered, hidden within the chambers of my murmuring heart. Sometimes I am able to muster enough time to say: *I shuffle through all the old letters that never reached you, the letters that never went beyond my dossier.* Sometimes I am able to confess: *I shuffle through in search of an answer, in search of a clue, secretly hoping to find the last number that you left me.*

Passages

It is shortly after midnight. What was Monday a few moments ago is now Tuesday on its way. It seems a strange idea that of names for each day, each passage of yet another night. . . . I have been concerning myself with passages of late, passages of light, of shadow, of love, of hate. Oh, how we mark the passages within our lives, noting the passing of time, of lives, of lovers, of loves, of relationships, to give pain an acceptable, palatable name – romantic, one might say.

Passages of hearts and minds and bodies and spirits – celestial and bruised. . . .

Rattling the bones

Beneath this bloated light
lying amid the bones
of thunder
my swollen tongue
from a different time
silent in its splendor
gags me.
I am sleepless days
and sleepless nights
at the mercy
of bloating heat
lying
amid the bones of thunder.

Jailer

This cage of flesh
and bone
needs cleaning.
The shadow of the jailer
looms behind me.

The Union

Your arbitrary rule of law
having been written
in my absence
I am
therefore
relegated
to the
rank and file

I have become
a shadow
in the corner
of your mind
I have become
once again
a living shadow
of your past

I have been
expunged
to the
back rooms
of the
non-negotiable

from the first time
to the
one-thousandth times
I have been
cast out
the window
as another
non-binding
non-negotiable
non-collective
agreement
torn to shreds

All negotiations
have failed

having bore
witness
to the gutting
of my inalienable rights

The marathon
has ended

having been
a slave
to this labour
I will cease
to bargain
at your table

having been
a commodity
to this labour
I shall
trade my heart
for shadows

This contract
is over

I hereby
give notice
of my intention
to invoke
notwithstanding
for this exclusion
this escape
from this labour

I stare
at the signature line
where it says
*the nameless shall
endorse here
having been executed
and bore witness
this contract shall
last in perpetuity
having been signed
and witnessed heretofor
with the understanding
that love and loyalty
from heretofor
shall just
be implied...*

I re-sign....

After the Solstice

The cold snap is supposed to be over. I've survived it well . . . the icy season. The solstice began on a hopeful wave of moonlight; a shift in the cycle of things.

It began a long time ago; a tiny murmur, a steady hum, until the bursting of a thousand tiny drums ended in a crescendo of crashing hearts. The path has been cold. Yet, in some indiscernible way, warm, uplifting, steady. . . even serene.

The crescendo was necessary, I suppose. As unstoppable as the cycle that accompanied the solstice, that will always accompany the solstice, the equinox, the solstice, the equinox again. The moon, the moon, the moon. The soft blue hands of the moon and the tenderness of hearts. It all began with the snow; then ice. The ice of the moon, the cold, cold ice of the moon . . . starting, beginning on the solstice. These words hard to release; not as easy as moonlight, as moonlight, as moonlight. This is my song to the moon.

There is a way to mark time. It all became easier to accept because it happened within a natural, powerful cycle of things, this cycle of things, cycle of things. Hearts moved on. The solstice of two hearts . . . two hearts. The solstice of many hearts. The ache does not have to mean devastation. It means I am alive.

I have watched the sun on consecutive afternoons cross the same part of the southern sky. I have watched it plainly; blue light on snow, captured in tiny crystals of ice. They have a life. There is no despair in ice. Like mirrors reflecting the light of the southern sky, or the moon high in the sky passing westward, the cycle reflects itself . . . myself. I need to let it pass; needing to allow the natural passage of things. I will allow it. The cold snap is over. I believe.

Memories crystallize into now, into light reflected into the future. That's where I am. Future light. I am reflected into the future. I am already alive tomorrow.

In the light of passing afternoons, the existence of sorrow is only a temporary necessity. It will not sustain me. It will not sustain my life. It is only temporary.

The solstice has passed; the sun is on its steady rise, bringing warmth and another sense of wholeness, of life, of light, of sustenance. I believe it. I believe it. I believe.

Hummingbird

I

The wind is strafing the landscape. Trees are barren reminders of what once was. Ice forms lightly on ponds and streams. Eagles slice the sky, riding invisible torrents and hurricanes beneath a deceiving blue. Migrating hawks soar and rise on unseen kettles of wind in an ever widening gyre of darkness. Now comes the journey home. Hummingbirds hum their way south. Their red throats coated with spring and summer nectar, their wings another revolution stronger. Take wing, little ones. Take wing. The temperature is dropping. The frost will soon turn into snow.

Tiny reassuring flutters echo in my inner ear. Signals of something coming. Someone on the edge of making contact. The hypnotic flutter of a thousand tiny feathers echo in my inner ear.

Inner rhythms remain muted. Stilled by the trials of hearts and thorns.

II

If the winds are horse spirits, their hooves are thundering by, impervious to rider and rein, stirrup and shoe. Visions that once crystallized now threaten to shudder and shatter beneath the thundering hooves of the wind. In the distance, a rider without a steed. Peace, a shadow of an uncompleted deed.

Somewhere a woman lights her pipe. Tobacco is sprinkled on the water and lights sparkle across her face. A small whirlwind prayer brushes over the ripples. *Please remember me. Please remember me.*

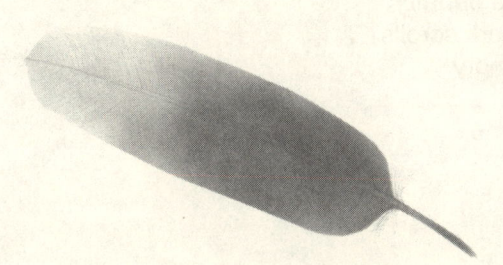

Migrations

Migrations

The migration song returned to us
We gathered berries for the journey
We wrapped your memories in safe bundles
We showed you the way on birchbark scrolls
We let the songs echo to your memory
We carried the sacred shell

In this land of Anishinaabe Akiing
We glimpse the blue flames
Ancestors leading us home
Ancestors leading us home

In this land of Anishinaabe Akiing
We glimpse the blue flames
Ancestors leading us home
Ancestors leading us home

We migrate through the stars
We dance with the northern lights
We migrate through stars
We dance with northern lights

Here upon Anishinaabe Earth
We glimpse the blue flames
Ancestors leading us
Ancestors leading us home

We let the songs echo to your memory
Across the land of Anishinaabe Akiing
Ancestors leading us home

Here upon Anishinaabe Earth
We glimpse the blue flames
And carried the sacred shell
Ancestors leading us home

We migrate through stars
We dance, we dance with northern lights
In this land of Anishinaabe Akiing
We glimpse the blue flames
Ancestors leading us, leading us home

We wrapped your memories for you in safe bundles
Throughout the land of Anishinaabe Akiing
Ancestors leading us home
Here upon Anishinaabe Earth
We glimpse the blue flames
We showed you the way on birchbark scrolls
Ancestors leading us, ancestors leading us home

We migrate through stars, we migrate
We dance, with northern lights we dance
In this land of the people's land
We glimpse the blue flames
Through the stars ancestors leading us home
The migration song returned to us
We dance with ancestors in northern lights
In this land of the people's land

Blue flames singing
Blue flames flickering across the land of
Anishinaabe Akiing
We gathered berries for the journey
We migrate with ancestors
Ancestors leading us home
The migration song returned to us
We gathered berries for the journey
We wrapped your memories in safe bundles
We showed you the way on birchbark scrolls
We let the songs echo to your memory
We carried the sacred shell

We carried the sacred shell
We carried the sacred shell
We carried the sacred shell

How long is your journey?
How strong is your song?
How strong is your journey?
How long is your song?
How long is your journey?
How strong is your song?
    How strong is your song?
       How strong is your song?
          How strong is your song?

Originally commissioned as part of a dramatic multi-media performance called *Migrations: The Eternal Journey* for the First Annual Native Educator's Conference, Thunder Bay, Ontario, November, 1993. *With thanks to Jim Dumont, Frank Montano & David Hopkins for their contributions of voice, song and interpretation for that original performance.*

Equinox II

Brave crows return before spring thaw
The air is changing
Winds are changing
The stars and constellations are changing too.

We still wait.

Somewhere the signal has been given
Notification has been served
A message has been sent to the sky people
The water people have sensed the vibrations
Winged ones have seen the semaphores
The flare of the sun in the east
The flare of the lights in the north.

They are coming home.

The trees have begun to shiver inside
Awakening the synapses
Freeing the jugular
The heart vein.

The roots have received word.

Recent Visitors

I have been glimpsing moments out of the corners of my eyes
While sitting, while travelling, while thinking
Something, someone, requires my attention.
I know not what nor whom it is.
I am not quick enough to see.
I am not quick enough to see.

Shoreline, tree line, waterline, skyline, heart line.
Not quick enough to see.

Shake the feathers

The leaves are singing changing songs for this new season. Their songs are punctuated by pale and bright yellows shaking to the beckoning winds that blow cooler. The sky sings the brightest blues. At night, the sky seems more alive with stars and constellations foretelling transformation, catharsis, and another revolution of changing songs. The trees stand a little taller after the spring and summer rains. Poplar and birch shiver and tremble in voices that lull the birds into silence. And when the birds do chatter and sing, their songs are travelling songs to show the way south. The monarchs have left Point Pelee to cross Lake Erie, continuing onward to the southern, butterfly nations. The dying plum and chokecherry leaves are pungent, red flags alongside the sumac and the maple. The wind changes, and the frost arrives under the cover of darkness. The more the earth changes, the more the earth remains the same.

Morning walks just after dawn and just before dusk reveal the subtle differences that may be missed with just the occasional glance. If one were to walk for the rest of one's days, past the same places day after day, the differences and perspectives would never be the same. It goes without saying, really. The sounds are different. There is a morning chorus, and there is an evening chorus. Each one is different, depending on the bird, the animal, the insect, or any of the other creatures that can make a sound. I've found myself wondering what would happen or what would be happening if the choruses of the morning and of the evening were to cease. What purpose do they serve? I've wondered about the call to prayers and the giving of thanks to the Creator that we are encouraged, asked, or told to do each day in order to continue to be a part of the earth's and of creation's perpetuation. Is this the purpose of the morning and evening choruses? If indeed it is, I have no doubts that the birds, the animals, the insects and all of the other creatures that can make a sound don't need the constant reminders that their human relatives need on a daily, repetitive basis. Perhaps that, in itself, is a reminder through the daily songs, the call to prayers and thanksgiving alive in the morning and evening choruses.

Walking through the woods, encountering the same hawk, the same animals, the same, quiet, blue heron, reminds me and causes me to ponder the notion of being a neighbour, a friend, a relative, sharing the same piece of land, drinking of the same water day after day, sleeping under the same expanse of sky night after night, dreaming. Dreaming.

I look at the leaves shaking, calling their medicines like rattles. I listen to the leaves shaking, speaking in one voice to the Creator. I look at the grass swaying, dancing to the beat of the Mother. I listen to the grass swaying, staying rooted to the Mother. I look at the birds singing, honouring the feathers on their backs. I listen to the birds singing, honouring the creation. I look at myself. I listen to myself. Shake the feathers!! Shake the feathers!!

Egress

Overcast skies, yellow leaves and grey splashing waters are the order for the day. Flocks of migrating geese have filled the skies with their incessant honking day and night. The sumacs are raging. The woods are brilliant patches of colour blending into the more subtle palettes of the surrounding fields. Migrating hawks, flocks of robins, blackbirds, and others, call and gather on their ever quickening journey south. Urgency permeates the air. An early winter? Early snows? The sky curtains the truth. At night, the stars sparkle and move in ribbons of undulating light all around the wild blue grin of the moon.

Spring Run

We wait for the frogs to sing
to announce spring run in the river
sucker, walleye, northern, sturgeon
swimming to that place
Poles need cutting
Nets need mending . . .

Cool night air
waiting for the tug
lifting the net with thighs as fulcrums
walleye flipping and flopping inside
swinging over, arcing over
flipping them into rock cracks
releasing full females back into the seething water
on their way to that place
swing back out
net resting in water
leaning on long cedar pole
messenger to your fingers, palms, arms
tensing thighs, lifting, turning, arcing over
swinging the next catch into rock fissure
heat of the fire touching your face
turning, resting the dip net mesh
just beneath the surface
heat of the fire at your back.

All through the night . . .
resting, lifting, swinging, arcing over
motion and movement, keeping time
tobacco smoke swirling at the edge of fire
at the edge of water, at the edge of light and darkness
burning over, arcing over, 10,000 years
to this night, this night of frogs singing
all of us
heading to that place. . . .

April Rising

The air is warming and the days are getting longer. The ground is beginning to peek through. Water is running in the creek. At night, the sound of flowing water is unmistakable. There is no interfering the sound. This morning, the same timbre held true. Today, rain is in the forecast. It will be welcomed. A sense of urgency and anticipation pulses through me like water breaking through ice. I want to walk the woods, to be in the midst of trees and the sounds and smells of this waking season. A lone goose flew over this morning, honking. In the subdued light of early morning, it was a wake up call to splendid light and creation.

The Way It Is

I

The veil of winter having been lifted,
warmth begins to return to the landscape.
Fingers of light from the sun reach out
to part tattered, grey curtains that undulate with the wind.

II

Grosbeaks, yellow ones, red ones, gather each morning to sing morning songs.
Finches, yellow ones, join in. Bluebirds, a pair of them, perch briefly in the poplars,
then flitter off. A hummingbird hovers briefly at an eastern window,
notification
having been served. . . .

Legacies

My mind has been on legacies lately,
imagining a child of the future wanting,
trying, to pass down
what has been handed down to him or her,
in their present, in their future,
from today, the past.

Will it be a vibrant,
crystalline-blue light
of energy and teachings,
fragile,
yet powerful to the touch?
Or will it be fragments
of a fractured, tiny goblet
spilled of our squandered visions?

Depending on where you stand –
so hard to tell, or really easy to predict. . . .

Still

We cull the light of the day through fragments of quartz and sky. The water in the river is muddy, though it moves swiftly. Spawning fish supposed to be on their spring run have not quite decided to do so with their usual spring gusto. Singing frogs have taken a long time to crawl out of the mud and muck; their songs echo across and from the beaver pond. The beavers have been slapping their tails on the water for about a week now; the impending danger or perceived threat has yet to make its appearance and presence known. Remnants of ice still flow on the lakes, rivers and creeks. Patches of snow still lie in the sheltered woods. Poplars have started to bud. Changes belie themselves in the air, in the land, in the waters, in the trees, and in the clouds. While the light seems fractured and obtuse, one could still see. While the river is muddy, it still runs swift. While the spring run seems sluggish, the fish still swim. While the frogs have been reluctant, their chorus is still strong. While the beavers have trepidation, they still dare to venture out of their lodges. Though the ice and snow leave slowly, green shoots still come through.

Dance of the Trees

A light snow covers the land. Grasses still manage to keep brown bristles above the margin of the snow. The birds of summer have left. The irreverent cacophony of crows has reached the pitch of silence in trees now bare. The doorway to winter has swung open. Another revolution begins.

Rhythms of a different sort reverberate and hum in muted songs of death, songs of death without the wails of mourning. Instead, a stream of welcoming songs grows steadily with each passing moon of winter. The blues of the translucent moon are almost touchable, almost reachable. . . . Almost.

The river still flows openly; the slow dance of water mingles with the steady advances of approaching cold fronts.

The trees shake and shiver vulnerably like bones in a rhythmic dissertation.
With the wind compose a mesmerizing symphony of breath and bone and light.

Altered
February 24, 1995

There really hasn't been that much snow.
Flocks of robins still danced in December.
Yesterday, the calls of crows was unnerving.
The river remains open in places while eagles fish at the edge of ice floes.
Last night, the northern lights danced wildly.
The bears will wake early; thunder will thunder in March.
It seems that there will not be much water.
It seems that the patterns of creation are changing with migrations forever altered.

Dream Horses

RedHawk, BlueSky, where have you gone?

A long time ago, according to the Elders, there were two families, the RedHawk Family and the BlueSky Family who once lived in my community of Manitou Rapids. Today, there are none of them left. They all died out, apparently, leaving no descendants. I wondered for many years about what that all meant. Where are the stories? I would wonder. I would ponder at length about the disappearance of those two families, and what legacies they might have left or continued had they survived. Inevitably, thinking of them and wondering about them, would make me think and wonder about the life and path that we are looking for as individuals, peoples, and communities, for the things that we need. Usually I have related this thinking and wondering to the search for those two families, seemingly forgotten, seemingly lost. And, in some way, still here. This poem and song cycle is dedicated to them, to my ancestors, to my relatives, to my Elders, and, to the children, who, someday will return.

I looked for red hawk
I looked for red hawk.

I looked into the sky
I looked into the sky.

I couldn't see red hawk.

There was no red hawk
There was no red hawk.

I looked for blue sky
I looked for blue sky.

I couldn't see blue sky.

There was no blue sky
There was no blue sky.

RedHawk, Blue Sky, where have you gone?
Where have you gone?
RedHawk, Blue Sky, where have you gone?
Where have you gone?

I see the horizon,
the horizon of trees
the horizon of trees
the horizon of trees.

I search the horizon for the red hawk
for the red hawk
for the red hawk
for the red hawk

There is no red hawk.   There is no red hawk.

I search the horizon for the blue sky
for the blue sky
for the blue sky
for the blue sky.

There is no blue sky.   There is no blue sky.

RedHawk, Blue Sky, where have you gone?
Where have you gone?
RedHawk, Blue Sky, where have you gone?
Where have you gone?

We lost our language
lost our language
lost our language
lost our language.

We lost our ceremonies
lost our ceremonies,
lost our ceremonies
lost our ceremonies.

Where have you gone?
Where have you gone?
Where have you gone?

RedHawk, Blue Sky, where have you gone?
Where have you gone?
RedHawk, Blue Sky, where have you gone?
Where have you gone?

We lost our dances
lost our dances
lost our dances
lost our dances.

Where have you gone?
Where have you gone?
Where have you gone?

RedHawk, Blue Sky, where have you gone?
Where have you gone?
RedHawk, Blue Sky, where have you gone?
Where have you gone?

We search for the women
search for the women
search for the women
search for the women.

Where have you gone?
Where have you gone?
Where have you gone?

RedHawk, Blue Sky, where have you gone?
Where have you gone?
RedHawk, Blue Sky, where have you gone?
Where have you gone?

We search for the warriors
search for the warriors
search for the warriors
search for the warriors.

Where have you gone?
Where have you gone?
Where have you gone?

RedHawk, Blue Sky, where have you gone?
Where have you gone?
RedHawk, Blue Sky, where have you gone?
Where have you gone?

We search for the children
search for the children
search for the children
search for the children.
Where have you gone?
Where have you gone?
Where have you gone?

RedHawk, Blue Sky, where have you gone?
Where have you gone?
RedHawk, Blue Sky, where have you gone?
Where have you gone?

Everywhere I look
Everywhere I look
Everywhere I look.

for the red hawk
for the red hawk
for the red hawk.

Everywhere I look
Everywhere I look
Everywhere I look.

for the blue sky
for the blue sky
for the blue sky

I am searching for myself,
searching for myself,
searching for myself,
searching for myself.

Where have you gone?
Where have you gone?
Where have you gone?

RedHawk, Blue Sky, where have you gone?
Where have you gone?
RedHawk, Blue Sky, where have you gone?
Where have you gone?

Voices in the sky
Voices in the sky
Voices in the sky.

Elders speak
Elders speak
Elders speak.

Children speak
Children speak
Children speak.

Dreamers speak
Dreamers speak
Dreamers speak.
I search the horizon for the red hawk
for the red hawk
for the red hawk
for the red hawk.

I search the horizon for the blue sky
for the blue sky
for the blue sky
for the blue sky.

Voices in the sky
Voices in the sky
Voices in the sky.

Here we are!
Here we are!
Here we are!
Here we are!
We are!
We are!
We are!
We are!
Here we are!
Here we are!
Here we are!
Here we are!

Here I am!
Here I am!
Here I am!
Here I am!
Here I am!
Here I am!
Here I am!
Here I am!

Language here! Language here! Language here! Language here!

Ceremonies here! Ceremonies here! Ceremonies here! Ceremonies here!

Dances here! Dances here! Dances here! Dances here!

Women here! Women here! Women here! Women here!

Warriors here! Warriors here! Warriors here! Warriors here!

Children here! Children here! Children here! Children here!
RedHawk, Blue Sky, where have you gone?
Where have you gone?
Where have you gone?
Where have you gone?

RedHawk, Blue Sky, where have you gone?
Where have you gone?
Where have you gone?
Where have you gone?

Seven Horses

Return to me, full circle, dream way, life way, message way, power way, healing way, beauty way, return to me . . .

While paddling a canoe, a man searches the shoreline for a figure in driftwood to which he would attach a poem, a prayer and tobacco for the friendship between him and another. Drifting along the shore, he passes a moose, a camel, and, finally, stops at the figure of a horse. The offering is made, the friendship lives on. . . .

Leaning against the wind, head down, a man unwillingly tired, seeking answers, seeking a place, seeking solace, on Gothenburg Road, in a heavy snowfall, comes face to face with a large, white horse standing in the middle of the road. Startled, he looks into his eyes and sees his own reflection, even in the blinding snow. Nowadays, he tirelessly draws faces in the manes of horses, hair blowing in the wind. . . .

A woman sits on a park bench in Montreal; a brown horse stands next to her to tell a story. She listens. As she turns away briefly, and upon turning back, the horse transformed into another who also dreams of horses. Upon waking each morning she now writes the stories down. . . .

Once, in a dream, as he was chasing a horse across the fields, two wolves intercepted and began to nip at its heels. He had a gun. His first inclination was to fire at the horse. Why? He did not know. While running across the fields, a bear loped out of the woods to join in the chase. He fired a shot into the cold, morning air. Upon hearing the shot and seeing him, the bear seemed frightened and dismayed, and then ran away. Finally, after catching up to the horse and the two wolves, the horse became calm, and the wolves transformed into his daughters. . . .

Somewhere near an old house, along an old road, across wide fields, another seeker rides a big horse in his dreams, white and grey, with wolves nipping at its heels. The bear in his dreams, stands watchful. . . .

Return to me, return to me, full circle, dream way, life way, message way, power way, healing way, beauty way, return to teach me, return to prepare me. . . .

Horsecoat

In memory of my Uncle Art
for making a boy smile.

A long time ago, my uncle would call me *Horsecoat*.
It was a nickname that he gave me.
One summer, when I was just a boy, I often wore a certain denim jacket;
colourful horses were embroidered on the front of each shoulder. They reminded me of rainbows.
Whenever I went to see my uncle, I wore them proudly, knowing he'd always say,
"Hey, Horsecoat! Where's Horsecoat? Are you Horsecoat?"
I remember smiles and laughter embroidered on faces,
horses and rainbows embroidered in time. . . .

Horsecoat ,
still here and still there,
through summers and years,
wearing well, though fading,
like denim, like boyhood,
embroidered in time,
like rainbows, like horses. . . .

Dream Horses

in memory of Walt Bresette

I

Beneath the moonlight, in the sky,
my dreams are horses
running south.

South is where the journey will end
and south is where it will begin again–
in the journey of the path of souls.

Along the southern trail,
there are side paths that lead into unknown places,
perhaps into box canyons or over the edge of hidden cliffs.
The horses do not go there.

Traveling for four days and four nights,
they will stop to eat at dawn,
drink from streams that carry water
clean and blue.

They will warm themselves at dusk and through each night
at ancient fires of memory and remembrance,
dreams of horses
that have passed this way before.

On the morning of the fifth day,
they will arrive at a river
that they will not need to ford.
Their hooves will carry them, dance
like diamonds across the surface of the water,
until they reach the southern shore,
where other dream horses gather,
to be reborn at the dawning of another day.

Oh, great rememberer, come back,
come back, into the lush, blue fields
of my dreams. . . .

II

You, with the blue heart–
gazing into fields where dreams lay fallow,
gather together, the mane of your horse,
turn him into the face
of the rising sun,
where the dew clings
to sweet, new grasses,
let him drink,
let him taste,
and then ride.

Publication Credits:

"In Neah Bay"
"After the Solstice"
appeared in Rampike, 2000

"Dream Horses"
appeared in Canadian Literature, 2000

"Spirit of Creation"
appeared in Celebration of Anishinaabe Achievers
of the Treaty #3 Nation
Commemorative Edition, March 2000.

"Ghosts on the rock"
appeared in Zenith City Arts